FRENCH
COOKBOOK

60 Recipes for Classic Food from France

Maki Blanc

© **Copyright 2022 by Maki Blanc- All rights reserved.**

This document is geared towards providing exact and reliable information in regard to the topic and issue covered. The publication is sold with the idea that the publisher is not required to render accounting, officially permitted, or otherwise, qualified services. If advice is necessary, legal or professional, a practiced individual in the profession should be ordered.

From a Declaration of Principles which was accepted and approved equally by a Committee of the American Bar Association and a Committee of Publishers and Associations.

In no way is it legal to reproduce, duplicate, or transmit any part of this document in either electronic means or in printed format. Recording of this publication is strictly prohibited and any storage of this document is not allowed unless with written permission from the publisher. All rights reserved.

The information provided herein is stated to be truthful and consistent, in that any liability, in terms of inattention or otherwise, by any usage or abuse of any policies, processes, or directions contained within is the solitary and utter responsibility of the recipient reader. Under no circumstances will any legal responsibility or blame be held against the publisher for any reparation, damages, or monetary loss due to the information herein, either directly or indirectly.

Respective authors own all copyrights not held by the publisher.

The information herein is offered for informational purposes solely and is universal as so. The presentation of the information is without contract or any type of guarantee assurance.

The trademarks that are used are without any consent, and the publication of the trademark is without permission or backing by the trademark owner.

All trademarks and brands within this book are for clarifying purposes only and are owned by the owners themselves, not affiliated with this document.

CONTENTS

INTRODUCTION 9

CHAPTER 1: TRADITIONAL PARIS AND ÎLE-DE-FRANCE RECIPES 12

    ILLE FLONTATE WITH FRESH CHERRIES 13

    MUSHROOMS IN WHITE WINE 14

    FRENCH MIMOSA 16

    FRENCH MACARONS 17

    FRENCH BAGUETTE 18

    SOUPE A LOIGNON 20

    LANGUE DE BOEUF 21

    OS A MOELLE 22

    FRENCH ESCARGOT 24

    CUISSES DE GRENOUILLES 26

CHAPTER 2: TRADITIONAL CHAMPAGNE, LORRAINE, AND ALSACE RECIPES 28

    KUGELHOPF WITH HONEYED MUSCAT PEARS 30

    SAUERKRAUT WITH PORK AND SAUSAGES 32

    PATE CHAMPENOIS 33

    ALSATIAN DUCK AND SAUERKRAUT 34

    CHOUCROUTE GARNIE 36

    SALAD DE PISSENLITS AU LARD 37

CHAPTER 3: TRADITIONAL NORMANDY, AND BRITTANY RECIPES 39

POULET A LA NORMANDE 40

FRENCH FISH STEW 42

GALLETE SAUCISSE 43

CREPES SALEES 44

FRENCH PATE 46

NORMANY PORK CASSEROLE WITH CIDER AND SMOKED BACON LARDONS 47

CHAPTER 4: TRADITIONAL LOIRE VALLEY AND CENTRAL FRANCE RECIPES 49

BLUEBERRY GALLETE 51

POMEGRANATE AND BALSAMIC STUFFED BUTTERNUT SQUASH 52

TOURA NOUGAT CAKE 54

BUBBLE TOP BROICHE 55

SAVOURY PALMIERS WITH PARMESAN AND BLACK PEPPER 56

THE SUZETTE SAUCE 57

CHAPTER 5: TRADITIONAL BURGUNDY AND FRANCHE-COMTÉ RECIPES 59

COQ AU VIN JAUNE 61

ESCALOPE DE VEAU COMTOISE 62

RACLETTE JURASSIENNE 64

POIRES AU VIN- WINE POACHED PEARS 65

TARTE AU GOUMEAU 66

CROUTE AU MÓNT DÓR 67

CHAPTER 6: TRADITIONAL BORDEAUX, PÉRIGORD, GASCONY, AND BASQUE COUNTRY RECIPES 69

BASQUE BRAISED CHICKEN WITH PEPPERS 71

BASQUE TUNA AND POTATO SOUP 72

BASQUE STYLE FISH WITH GREEN PEPPERS AND MANILA CLAMS 74

CANÉLE RECIPE 75

CREAM PUFF 76

SAINT EMILION MACARON 78

LE PETIT SALE 80

FRENCH BISTRO SALAD 81

CHERRY CLAFOUTIS 82

SASKATOON CLAFOUTIS 83

CHAPTER 7: TRADITIONAL PROVENCE-ALPES-CÔTE D'AZUR RECIPES 85

PROVENCAL BEEF STEW 87

FRENCH ANCHOIADE 88

SWEET CHARD PIE 89

SOCCA NICOISE FLATBREAD 90

AUBERGINE & COURGETTE TIAN 92

SPINACH BAKE 94

VAUCLUSE TROUT 95

FRESH FRENCH GOAT CHEESE DIP 96

POTATO AND MINT RAVIOLI 97

LARDON AND OLIVE CAKE 98

CHAPTER 8: TRADITIONAL CORSICA RECIPES 101

CORSICAN VEAL AND OLIVE STEW 102

CANNELLONI BROCCIU 103

CORSICAN LEMON CHEESECAKE 104

CORSICAN OMELETTE 105

CORSICAN BISCUITS 106

MUSHROOM PATE 108

CONCLUSION 110

Introduction

French food is famous for its delicacy as well as its effortlessness. French food has attained a royal image because of its fundamental fixings and respected procedures that are usually intended for both effectiveness and unique style.

France is the zenith of culinary sentiment and gastronomical extravagance, eminent for its refinement as well as its straightforwardness. The easy class of French food comes from a couple of fundamental fixings and respected methods that have impacted the vast majority of the culinary styles we use today, from the Haute cooking of Paris to the organic products from the Mediterranean ocean.

Cooking from the north of France will, in general, incline toward the velvety lavishness of margarine, while the south France is inclined towards using olive oil in their recipes. Utilize unsalted butter, so you have flavor and health at the same time. The French add a handle of margarine towards the end of making a sauce to give it added profundity and an excellent sparkle. Olive oil is additionally the staple element of many sauces, for example, aioli, mayonnaise, and French dressing. No soup or larder is made without olive oil in France.

Garlic is possibly the most renowned of French fixings and arrives in an assortment of flavors, i.e. smoked, dark, cured. You can add garlic to escargots with parsley, spread, and shallots. You could make garlic soup on the off chance that you would not fret possessing a scent like garlic for quite a while! Dijon mustard is adaptable and not only used as a sauce but is also added in different recipes. Add a teaspoon to a skillet of vegetables seared in butter or to a chicken meal. It provides everything with an additional punch of flavor.

Crème fraîche is a soured cream. Yet, it contains no additional thickeners and will, in general, have a higher fat substance. It is helpful in sauces, goulashes, and puddings or can be spooned into natural products for a lovely sweet taste. On the off chance that you cannot find any at the grocery store, you can also start making your own. Clearly, nothing beats fresh spices, however; it merits having a few dried choices (Herbs de Provence) in hand as well, as they function admirably in slow-cooked dishes like meals and soups.

This book contains 60 delicious recipes belonging to different cities of France. The recipes are categorized as belonging to Paris, Île-de-France, Champagne, Lorraine, Alsace, Normandy, Brittany, Loire Valley, Central France, Burgundy, Franche-Comté, Bordeaux, Périgord, Gascony, Basque country, Provence-Alpes-Côte d'Azur, and Corsica recipes. You are all ready to cook authentic French food with this cookbook by your side. So, keep reading!

Chapter 1: Traditional Paris and Île-de-France Recipes

The best food sources in Paris are generally incredibly popular French dishes that merit incredible taste. These exemplary plans will ease up even the gloomiest of days because of their exceptional preferences and flavors. Paris, the City of Light, is legitimately celebrated for its food, which has been sent out to each corner of the globe. Paris has something delectable for everybody. Food from Île-de-France is undeniably popular and profoundly respected. In certain cafés, you will track down the best, freshest fixings. A large part of the produce sold in the city's markets has been grown on the encompassing rich farmland. Follow the recipes below to make delicious food at home:

ILLE FLONTATE WITH FRESH CHERRIES

INGREDIENTS

- **For the meringue:**
- One cup of icing sugar
- Two egg whites
- One cup of sugar
- One teaspoon of cherry essence
- Pralines for serving
- Salt to taste
- **For the custard:**
- One vanilla pod
- One cup of pitted cherries
- Two cups of milk
- Five egg yolk
- Half cup of sugar

COOK TIME: 20 mins
SERVING: 4

INSTRUCTIONS

1. Take a large pan.
2. Add the milk, pitted cherries and sugar into the pan.
3. Mix the ingredients well and add the eggs yolk and vanilla pod into the pan.
4. Mix all the ingredients well to form a thick custard.
5. Pour the custard into a bowl when done.
6. Take a large bowl.
7. Add the egg whites, cherry essence and salt into the bowl.
8. Beat the egg whites well and then add the icing sugar into the bowl.
9. Beat the mixture well until the eggs turn stiff.
10. Add the meringue on top of the custard with the help of a pipping bag.
11. Take a pan.
12. Add the sugar into the pan.
13. Melt the sugar.
14. Cook the sugar well and then use a spoon to add the melted sugar on the meringue.
15. Add the pralines on top of the melted sugar.
16. Your dish is ready to be served.

MUSHROOMS IN WHITE WINE

INGREDIENTS

- A quarter cup of Two pounds of mushroom slices
- Two tablespoons of minced garlic
- One tablespoon of olive oil
- One teaspoon of Italian seasoning
- A quarter cup of dry white wine
- Salt to taste
- Black pepper to taste
- A pinch of nutmeg
- Two tablespoons of chopped chives

COOK TIME: *15 mins*
SERVING: *6*

INSTRUCTIONS

1. Take a sauce pan.
2. Add the olive oil and minced garlic into the pan.
3. Cook the minced garlic well until the garlic turns fragrant.
4. Add the mushroom slices into the pan.
5. Cook the mushrooms well.
6. Add the salt, black pepper and dry white wine into the pan.
7. Cook the mixture well for about ten minutes.
8. Add the Italian seasonings and nutmeg into the sauce pan.
9. Cook well.
10. Dish out the mushrooms.
11. Garnish the dish with chopped chives.
12. Your dish is ready to be served.

FRENCH MIMOSA

INGREDIENTS

- One cup of dry champagne
- Two tablespoons of freshly chopped raspberries
- Four cups of sparkling water
- One cup of ice cubes
- Half cup of chambord

COOK TIME: 0 *mins*
SERVING: 2

INSTRUCTIONS

1. Take a blender.
2. Add the sparkling water, raspberries, dry champagne, chambord and ice cubes into the blender.
3. Blend everything well.
4. Pour the mimosa into glasses.
5. The dish is ready to be served.

FRENCH MACARONS

INGREDIENTS

- One cup of almond flour
- A quarter teaspoon of cream of tartar
- One cup of superfine sugar
- Two drops of gel food color
- One cup of egg whites
- Salt to taste
- One teaspoon of vanilla extract
- One cup of icing sugar
- Black pepper to taste
- One cup of macaroon filling

COOK TIME: 20 mins
SERVING: 4

INSTRUCTIONS

1. Take a large bowl.
2. Add the egg whites, and salt into a bowl.
3. Beat the egg whites well until they turn stiff.
4. Add the icing sugar, vanilla extract, gel color, cream of tartar and superfine sugar into the bowl.
5. Mix all the ingredients well to form a homogenous mixture.
6. Add the almond flour slowly into the egg whites' mixture.
7. Fold the mixture well.
8. Preheat the oven at 180 degrees.
9. Take a greased baking tray.
10. Pour the macaron mixture into a pipping bag
11. Make small cookies on the baking tray.
12. Place the baking tray into the oven.
13. Bake the macarons for twenty minutes.
14. Dish out the macarons when done.
15. Let the macarons cool down.
16. Add the macaron filling on top of the macaron.
17. Add another macaron on top to form a macaron sandwich.
18. Your dish is ready to be served.

FRENCH BAGUETTE

INGREDIENTS

- One cup of water
- One teaspoon of salt
- Two and a half cup of flour
- One and a half teaspoon of yeast
- One tablespoon of sugar
- One tablespoon of water
- One egg yolk

COOK TIME: 15 mins
SERVING: 6

INSTRUCTIONS

1. Take a dough mixer.
2. Add the sugar, yeast, flour and salt into the mixer.
3. Mix well.
4. Add the water, egg yolk and let the ingredients mix well until the dough is done.
5. Cover the bowl for about thirty minutes.
6. You will notice the dough rising.
7. Press the dough down making sure no air spaces are left inside.
8. Remove from the bowl and cut the dough into two.
9. Shape the dough into log structures.
10. Take a baking tray.
11. Grease the tray well and place the logs on the tray.
12. Cut down any shapes or designs on the dough with the help of a blade.
13. Let the dough rise again for thirty to forty minutes.
14. Brush the top with egg yolk and water mixture.
15. Place it in an oven for about twenty-five to thirty minutes.
16. Make sure the oven is preheated before you place your dough in it.
17. Dish out the bread when the exterior turn light golden brown in color.
18. Let the bread cool down and then serve.

SOUPE A LOIGNON

INGREDIENTS

- Two cups of chicken stock
- Two crushed garlic
- A pinch of salt
- A pinch of black pepper
- Two tablespoons of olive oil
- One cup of dried white wine
- One cup of onion
- T tablespoons of all-purpose flour
- Two tablespoons of Worcestershire sauce
- T tablespoons of softened butter
- One bay leaf
- Two tablespoons of fresh thyme
- One cup of grated or sliced gruyere cheese
- French bread slices
- One cup of chopped dill

COOK TIME: *20 mins*
SERVING: *4*

INSTRUCTIONS

1. Take a large saucepan.
2. Add the oil and onions into the pan.
3. Cook the onions until they turn golden brown.
4. Add the crushed garlic into the pan.
5. Add the spices into the mixture.
6. Add the all-purpose flour, Worcestershire sauce and dried white wine.
7. Add the butter and then add the chicken stock.
8. Cover the pan with a lid for five minutes.
9. Let the soup cook properly.
10. Dish out the soup into soup bowls.
11. Add the bread slices on top of the soup.
12. Add the sliced cheese on top.
13. Bake the soup for ten minutes.
14. Switch off the oven when the cheese melts.
15. Add the chopped fresh dill on top.
16. The dish is ready to be served.

LANGUE DE BOEUF

INGREDIENTS

- One and a half pound of beef tongue pieces
- Two tablespoons of chopped garlic
- One bay leaf
- One tablespoon of chopped thyme
- One cup of chopped tomatoes
- A quarter cup of chopped leeks
- Five cups of water
- One tablespoon of chopped parsley
- One teaspoon of salt
- One tablespoon of black pepper
- A large chopped onion
- One pound of lentils
- A quarter cup of olive oil

COOK TIME: *70 mins*
SERVING: *4*

INSTRUCTIONS

1. Take a large saucepan.
2. Add the olive oil into the pan.
3. Add the beef tongue pieces into the pan.
4. Cook the beef well and dish out when done.
5. Add the onions and garlic into the pan.
6. Cook well.
7. Add the leeks into the pan.
8. Add the lentils, tomatoes, thyme, bay leaf water, salt and black pepper into the pan.
9. Mix well.
10. Cook the dish for about twenty minutes.
11. Add the chopped parsley on top of the dish.
12. The dish is ready to be served.

OS A MOELLE

INGREDIENTS

- Two tablespoons of olive oil
- Four large bones with bone marrow
- Two tablespoons of Dijon mustard
- One cup of white wine
- Salt to taste
- Black pepper to taste
- Half cup of brandy
- One cup of any stock
- A quarter cup of red wine
- One tablespoons of dried thyme

COOK TIME: 30 mins
SERVING: 4

INSTRUCTIONS

1. Take a large pan to make sure the bones fit in.
2. You can reduce the size of the bone if a large pan is unavailable.
3. Add the olive oil into the pan.
4. Add the bones and thyme into the pan.
5. Cook well.
6. Add the red wine, brandy, salt and black pepper into the pan.
7. Add the white wine, stock and Dijon mustard into the pan.
8. Cook the bone pieces for twenty minutes.
9. Dish out when done.
10. Your dish is ready to be served.

FRENCH ESCARGOT

INGREDIENTS

- Two tablespoons of unsalted butter
- One cup of chopped shallots
- One pound of snails
- One cup of chicken stock
- Half cup of thyme
- Half cup of rosemary
- A pinch of salt
- A pinch of black pepper
- Half teaspoon of fennel seeds
- Half cup of red wine
- Half cup of parsley sauce
- Toasted bread slices for serving

COOK TIME: *30 mins*
SERVING: *4*

INSTRUCTIONS

1. Take a large pan.
2. Add the unsalted butter into the pan.
3. Add the snails into the pan.
4. Cook the snails well.
5. Add the rosemary, thyme, parsley sauce, and red wine into the pan.
6. Cook the ingredients well.
7. Add the shallots into the pan.
8. Add the chicken stock into the pan.
9. Cook the ingredients well.
10. Place a lid on top of the pan.
11. Cook the snails for ten to fifteen minutes.
12. Dish out when the sauce turns thick.
13. Your dish is ready to be served.

CUISSES DE GRENOUILLES

INGREDIENTS

- Two tablespoons of butter
- One cup of chicken stock
- One tablespoon of cognac
- One pound of frogs legs
- Half teaspoon of allspice
- Two bay leaves
- A pinch of salt
- A pinch of black pepper
- Half teaspoon of fennel seeds
- Half cup of red wine vinegar
- Half tablespoon of chopped ginger

COOK TIME: *30 mins*
SERVING: *4*

INSTRUCTIONS

1. Take a large pan.
2. Add the butter into the pan.
3. Add the frog legs into the pan.
4. Cook the frog legs well.
5. Add the bay leaves, salt, black pepper, fennel seeds, cognac and allspice into the pan.
6. Cook the ingredients well.
7. Add the chopped garlic into the pan.
8. Add the ginger, red wine vinegar, and chicken stock into the pan.
9. Cook the ingredients well.
10. Place a lid on top of the pan.
11. Cook the frog for ten to fifteen minutes.
12. Dish out when the frog is done.
13. Your dish is ready to be served.

Chapter 2: Traditional Champagne, Lorraine, and Alsace Recipes

The gastronomy of Alsace-Lorraine, an area in Northeast France, is ideally suited for every season! The fixings and dishes invoke comfort food in abundance to appreciate in your comfortable fall sweater. The land that makes up Alsace-Lorraine has been passed to and fro among Germany and France throughout the long term. The Champagne food and gastronomy are an ideal illustration of exquisite French cuisine! With its delectable items from the Champagne woods like mushrooms and wild game and its fine neighborhood cheddar, including the notable French Brie, this Northern locale of France has numerous culinary gems on offer. That might clarify why it is viewed as one of the supports of French gastronomy! Following are some amazing recipes you need to follow:

KUGELHOPF WITH HONEYED MUSCAT PEARS

INGREDIENTS

- One cup of sliced almonds
- Half cup of butter
- Two cups of heavy cream
- One teaspoon of vanilla extract
- Two cups of all-purpose flour
- Half cup of white sugar
- Six egg yolks
- A pinch of salt
- One cup of dried raisins
- **For the honey Muscat pears:**
- Two tablespoons of honey
- One cup of white wine
- Two cups of caster sugar
- A quarter teaspoon of cinnamon powder
- Six pears

COOK TIME: 40 mins
SERVING: 6

INSTRUCTIONS

1. Take a large bowl.
2. Add the butter, heavy cream, egg yolks and white sugar into the bowl.
3. Mix all the ingredients well to form a homogenous mixture.
4. Add the flour, salt, vanilla extract slowly into the egg yolks mixture.
5. Add the almond slices and raisins into the cake mixture.
6. Fold the mixture well.
7. Preheat the oven at 180 degrees.
8. Take a greased baking tray.
9. Add the cake mixture into the tray.
10. Place the baking tray into the oven.
11. Bake the cake for forty minutes.
12. Dish out the cake when done.
13. Take a pan.
14. Add the caster sugar, white wine, honey and cinnamon powder into the pan.
15. Let the mixture cook well until the sugar starts melting.
16. Add the pears into the honey mixture.
17. Coat the honey sauce all over the pears.
18. Switch off the stove.
19. Cut the cake into slices.
20. Transfer the slices and honey pears into serving plates.
21. Your dish is ready to be served.

SAUERKRAUT WITH PORK AND SAUSAGES

INGREDIENTS

- Two tablespoons of butter
- One tablespoon of cognac
- Two cups of pork pieces
- Half teaspoon of allspice
- Two tablespoons of brown sugar
- One cup of sausage slices
- Two bay leaf
- A pinch of salt
- One cup of sauerkraut pieces
- A pinch of black pepper
- Half cup of apple cider vinegar
- One cup of chopped onion
- Half tablespoon of chopped garlic and ginger

COOK TIME: 40 mins
SERVING: 6

INSTRUCTIONS

1. Take a large pan.
2. Add the butter into the pan.
3. Add the pork pieces, chopped onion, ginger and garlic into the pan.
4. Cook the ingredients well.
5. Add the brown sugar, bay leaves, salt, black pepper, sauerkraut pieces, sausage slices, cognac and allspice into the pan.
6. Cook the ingredients well.
7. Add the apple cider vinegar into the pan.
8. Cook the ingredients well.
9. Place a lid on top of the pan.
10. Cook the meat pieces for ten to fifteen minutes.
11. Dish out when the meat is done.
12. Your dish is ready to be served.

PATE CHAMPENOIS

INGREDIENTS

- Two tablespoons of olive oil
- Two teaspoons of chopped garlic
- One cup of pork meat
- One cup of rabbit meat
- One cup of sausage mince
- Four large pastry sheets
- One cup of marc de champagne
- Half cup of chicken stock
- Salt to taste
- Black pepper to taste
- One teaspoon of de beurre
- Two tablespoons of chopped onions
- One teaspoon of espelette pepper

COOK TIME: 30 mins
SERVING: 4

INSTRUCTIONS

1. Take a pan.
2. Add the olive oil, and onions into the pan.
3. Cook the onions until they turn soft.
4. Add the minced garlic, pork meat, rabbit meat, and sausage mince into the pan.
5. Cook well.
6. Add the marc de champagne, espelette pepper, de beurre, salt and black pepper into the pan.
7. Cook the ingredients well and add the chicken stock into the pan.
8. Cook the chicken pieces for ten minutes.
9. Dish out when done.
10. Cut the pastry sheets in half.
11. Stuff the formed mixture on the pastry sheets.
12. Roll the pasty sheets and close the opened ends with a fork
13. Place the pastries on a greased baking dish.
14. Bake the pastries for thirty minutes.
15. Dish out when the pastries turn golden brown in color.
16. Your dish is ready to be served.

ALSATIAN DUCK AND SAUERKRAUT

INGREDIENTS

- One and a half pound of duck pieces
- Six garlic cloves
- One bay leaf
- One tablespoon of chopped thyme
- One cup of buttermilk
- One cup of sauerkraut slices
- One tablespoon of chopped parsley
- One teaspoon of salt
- One tablespoon of black pepper
- A large sliced onion
- A quarter cup of olive oil
- Half teaspoon of grated nutmeg
- One and a half cup of cream

COOK TIME: 70 mins
SERVING: 4

INSTRUCTIONS

1. Take a large saucepan.
2. Add the olive oil into the pan.
3. Add the onions and garlic into the pan.
4. Cook well.
5. Add the duck pieces into the pan.
6. Add the salt, nutmeg, bay leaf, sauerkraut slices, cream, and black pepper into the pan.
7. Mix well.
8. Simmer the ingredients and add the buttermilk, and thyme for fifty minutes and then dish out.
9. Make sure all the sauce is dried properly.
10. Add the chopped parsley on top of the duck and sauerkraut.
11. The dish is ready to be served.

CHOUCROUTE GARNIE

INGREDIENTS

- Two tablespoons of butter
- One tablespoon of cognac
- Two cups of bacon pieces
- Half teaspoon of allspice
- Two tablespoons of brown sugar
- One cup of ham slices
- One cup of pork chops
- One cup of chicken stock
- Two bay leaf
- Half pound of golden potatoes
- A pinch of salt
- One cup of sauerkraut pieces
- A pinch of black pepper
- Half cup of dry white wine
- One cup of chopped onion
- Two tablespoons of brandy

COOK TIME: *30 mins*
SERVING: *4*

INSTRUCTIONS

1. Take a large pan.
2. Add the butter into the pan.
3. Add the pork chops, chopped onion, golden potatoes, bacon and ham into the pan.
4. Cook the ingredients well.
5. Add the dry white wine, brown sugar, bay leaves, salt, black pepper, sauerkraut pieces, sausage slices, cognac and allspice into the pan.
6. Cook the ingredients well.
7. Add the chicken stock into the pan.
8. Cook the ingredients well.
9. Place a lid on top of the pan.
10. Cook the meat pieces for ten to fifteen minutes.
11. Dish out when the meat is done and water is completely dried.
12. Your dish is ready to be served.

SALAD DE PISSENLITS AU LARD

INGREDIENTS

- Three cups of dandelion leaves
- One cup of bacon slices
- Half cup of fresh thyme
- Half teaspoon of smoked paprika
- Half cup of chopped celery
- Two tablespoons of olive oil
- Two tablespoons of honey
- Half cup of Dijon mustard

COOK TIME: *10 mins*
SERVING: *2*

INSTRUCTIONS

1. Take a pan.
2. Add the olive oil and bacon into the pan.
3. Cook the bacon well.
4. Dish out when the bacon is done.
5. Take a large bowl.
6. Add the honey, Dijon mustard, and paprika into a bowl.
7. Mix all the ingredients well to form a homogenous mixture.
8. Add the cooked bacon, dandelion leaves, fresh thyme and chopped celery on top of the mixture.
9. Toss the salad to make sure everything is mixed properly.
10. Your dish is ready to be served.

Chapter 3: Traditional Normandy, and Brittany Recipes

Normandy offers an astonishing and top-notch gastronomical assortment. First comes its lavish fish: shellfish from the untamed ocean. Also, for each significant town, there is probably a forte. Then, let us not fail to remember those extraordinary Normandy cows, who give milk in excess and the cheese produced using the milk. Lastly, regarding organic products, Normandy holds the expert. They are utilized in making juice and the delicious calvados. The cooking of Brittany is profoundly rooted in a lifestyle that was one of the most unfortunate in France, and the food of Brittany depends on what is fished from the ocean and filled in its rich valleys. Breton food is joined by astonishing wines, the exceptionally customary neighborhood Breton Ciders, and a couple of incredible Breton brews. You will definitely love the recipes below.

POULET A LA NORMANDE

INGREDIENTS

- Two tablespoons of olive oil
- Two teaspoons of chopped garlic
- One cup of honey crisp apples
- Two tablespoons of corn starch
- Half cup of hard cider vinegar
- Salt to taste
- Black pepper to taste
- Half cup of crème fraiche
- Two tablespoons of chopped pearl onions
- Two chicken fillets
- A quarter cup of brandy
- One tablespoons of dried thyme

COOK TIME: *20 mins*
SERVING: *4*

INSTRUCTIONS

1. Take a pan.
2. Add the olive oil, and onions into the pan.
3. Cook the onions until they turn soft.
4. Add the minced garlic, chicken pieces and honey crisp apple slices into the pan.
5. Cook well.
6. Add the dried thyme, brandy, salt and black pepper into the pan.
7. Add the hard cider vinegar, and crème fraiche into the pan.
8. Cook the duck pieces for ten minutes.
9. Dish out when done.
10. Your dish is ready to be served.

FRENCH FISH STEW

INGREDIENTS

- Two strips of orange peel
- Three bay leaves
- One cup of chopped onions
- One tablespoon of black pepper
- One cup of chopped leek
- Two tablespoons of olive oil
- Two teaspoons of chopped garlic
- One cup of mussels
- One cup of mixed Mediterranean fish
- One cup of tomato paste
- One tablespoon of harissa
- One teaspoon of black pepper
- Two cups of ripe tomatoes
- Two cups of fish stock
- Half cup of mayonnaise
- One Star anise
- A pinch of salt
- One tablespoon of chopped fresh chives

COOK TIME: *20 mins*
SERVING: *4*

INSTRUCTIONS

1. Take a large pan.
2. Add the oil and onions into the pan.
3. Cook the onions until they turn soft and translucent.
4. Add the garlic into the pan.
5. Cook the mixture well.
6. Add the tomato paste, chopped ripe tomatoes and spices.
7. Cook the mixture for five minutes.
8. Add the mussels, and Mediterranean fish into the pan.
9. Cook the ingredients well.
10. Add the fish stock, harissa, chopped leeks, mayonnaise and orange peel.
11. Cover the pan and cook for ten minutes.
12. Garnish the dish with chopped fresh chives.
13. Your dish is ready to be served.

GALLETE SAUCISSE

INGREDIENTS

- Two and a quarter teaspoon of active yeast
- One cup of water
- Two and a half cup of all-purpose flour
- One teaspoon of sugar
- Two tablespoons of olive oil
- One tablespoon of sea salt
- One cup of caramelized onion paste
- Two cups of Gruyere cheese
- Four sausages

COOK TIME: *20 mins*
SERVING: *4*

INSTRUCTIONS

1. Take a mixing bowl.
2. Add the all-purpose flour, sugar, active yeast and sea salt into the bowl.
3. Mix well and then add the olive oil and water into the bowl.
4. Knead the dough well and place it aside for thirty to forty minutes.
5. Make four small balls from the dough.
6. Roll out the balls into semi thick sheets.
7. Add the caramelized onion paste, sausage and Gruyere cheese on the rolled dough.
8. Now roll the dough to tuck in the onion mixture and sausage inside.
9. Preheat the oven at 180 degrees.
10. Place the rolled galette on a greased and lined up baking tray.
11. Bake the rolled galette for twenty to thirty minutes or until it turns golden brown.
12. Dish out when done.
13. Your dish is ready to be served.

CREPES SALEES

INGREDIENTS

- Two tablespoons of creamy softened butter
- One cup of all-purpose flour
- Two tablespoons of milk
- Two large eggs
- One teaspoon of vanilla extract
- A quarter cup of cream cheese
- One cup of chopped and cooked ham
- Black pepper to taste
- Salt to taste

COOK TIME: *15 mins*
SERVING: *3*

INSTRUCTIONS

1. Take a bowl.
2. Add the creamy softened butter into the bowl.
3. Add in the all-purpose flour, milk, vanilla extract, and eggs.
4. Mix the ingredients carefully.
5. Add the mixture in small quantities in a pan.
6. Let the crepes turn golden on both sides.
7. Dish out the crepes when done.
8. Take a bowl.
9. Add the cream cheese, salt, black pepper and ham into the bowl.
10. Mix the ingredients well.
11. Add the ham mixture on the crepe.
12. Roll the crepes into a sandwich.
13. Dish out.
14. Your dish is ready to be served.

FRENCH PATE

INGREDIENTS

- Two tablespoons of butter
- Two cups of chicken liver mince
- Half teaspoon of thyme
- Two bay leaf
- A pinch of salt
- One teaspoon of nutmeg
- A pinch of black pepper
- Half cup of brandy
- One cup of chopped onion
- Half tablespoon of chopped garlic

COOK TIME: *30 mins*
SERVING: *4*

INSTRUCTIONS

1. Take a large pan.
2. Add the butter into the pan.
3. Add the onions and liver mince into the pan.
4. Cook the meat well.
5. Add the bay leaves, salt, black pepper, and thyme into the pan.
6. Cook the ingredients well.
7. Add the chopped garlic into the pan.
8. Add the brandy into the pan.
9. Cook the ingredients well.
10. Place a lid on top of the pan.
11. Cook the mixture for ten to fifteen minutes.
12. Dish out when the meat is done.
13. Your dish is ready to be served.

NORMANY PORK CASSEROLE WITH CIDER AND SMOKED BACON LARDONS

INGREDIENTS

- One tablespoon of Dijon mustard
- One tablespoon of chopped fresh chives
- Half teaspoon of smoked paprika
- One cup of pork pieces
- One cup of gruyere cheese
- Two tablespoons of apple cider vinegar
- Two tablespoons of olive oil
- One cup of dried white wine
- Half cup of milk
- One cup of bacon lardons
- One teaspoon of herb powder
- One cup of onion
- One teaspoon of chopped garlic

COOK TIME: 30 mins
SERVING: 4

INSTRUCTIONS

1. Take a pan.
2. Add in the oil and onions.
3. Cook the onions until they become soft and fragrant.
4. Add the spices.
5. Mix the ingredients carefully and cover the pan.
6. Mix the bacon lardons, pork pieces, apple cider vinegar and dry white wine into the mixture.
7. Cook the chicken well.
8. Switch off the stove.
9. Add the rest of the ingredients into it when the mixture cools down.
10. Pour the casserole mixture in a baking dish.
11. Sprinkle the shredded gruyere cheese on top.
12. Bake the casserole for twenty minutes.
13. Dish out the casserole when done.
14. Sprinkle the cilantro on top.
15. Your dish is ready to be served.

Chapter 4: Traditional Loire Valley and Central France Recipes

A dash of ingenuity, a dash of tradition, a pinch of audacity, and a dash of know-how: combine well to produce an excellent definition of Centre Loire Valley cuisine. Prepare the gourmet in you for a parade of flavors as you travel through our region. Fine dining is a way of life here. The Loire food is wealthy in flavors. White and green asparagus, Nantes sheep's lettuce, leeks, cherries, radishes, artichokes, apples, button mushrooms, strawberries, and numerous different leafy foods are usually eaten in both the cities. Follow the recipes below to indulge in the flavors of these two cities.

BLUEBERRY GALLETE

INGREDIENTS

- Two and a quarter teaspoon of active yeast
- One cup of water
- Two and a half cup of all-purpose flour
- One teaspoon of sugar
- Two tablespoons of olive oil
- One tablespoon of sea salt
- Half cup of granulated sugar
- One teaspoon of corn starch
- Two tablespoons of lemon juice
- One cup of blueberries

COOK TIME: 20 *mins*
SERVING: 4

INSTRUCTIONS

1. Take a mixing bowl.
2. Add the all-purpose flour, sugar, active yeast and sea salt into the bowl.
3. Mix well and then add the olive oil and water into the bowl.
4. Knead the dough well and place it aside for thirty to forty minutes.
5. Make four small balls from the dough.
6. Roll out the balls into semi thick sheets.
7. Take a small bowl.
8. Add the granulated sugar, lemon juice, blueberries and corn starch into the bowl.
9. Add the blueberry mixture on the flattened round rolled dough.
10. Preheat the oven at 180 degrees.
11. Place the galette on a greased and lined up baking tray.
12. Bake the galette for twenty to thirty minutes or until it turns golden brown.
13. Dish out when done.
14. Your dish is ready to be served.

POMEGRANATE AND BALSAMIC STUFFED BUTTERNUT SQUASH

INGREDIENTS

- One pound of ground beef
- Two tablespoons of minced garlic
- Half cup of dry white wine
- Half cup of cilantro
- Two tablespoons of olive oil
- One tablespoon of dried rosemary
- Half teaspoon of salt
- One cup of sliced shallots
- One teaspoon of black pepper
- One teaspoon of dried thyme
- Two tablespoons of apple cider vinegar
- Half teaspoon of smoked paprika
- One cup of pomegranate seeds
- Two medium sized butternut

COOK TIME: 50 mins
SERVING: 4

INSTRUCTIONS

1. Take a large pan.
2. Add the olive oil into it.
3. Add the shallots into the pan and cook until they turn soft.
4. Add the garlic, ground beef and dry white wine in the pan.
5. Cook the beans in the wine for five to ten minutes.
6. Add the rosemary, apple cider vinegar, salt, black pepper, thyme, and paprika into the mixture.
7. Cook for ten minutes and then dish out.
8. Cut the butternut squash in half.
9. Clean the squash and stuff the cooked beef mixture into the squash.
10. Bake the squash for about fifteen minutes at 180 degrees.
11. Dish out when done.
12. Garnish the dish with cilantro and pomegranate seeds.
13. Your dish is ready to be served.

TOURA NOUGAT CAKE

INGREDIENTS

- Two cups of any fruit slices
- Half cup of apple jam
- Half cup of icing sugar
- Two cups of sugar
- A pack of tart dough
- One cup of almond meal
- Half cup of lemon juice

COOK TIME: *30 mins*
SERVING: *4*

INSTRUCTIONS

1. Preheat the oven at 180 degrees.
2. Take a large bowl.
3. Add the almond meal, apple jam, fruit slices, lemon juice and sugar into the bowl.
4. Lay the tart dough into greased tart dishes.
5. Add the almond meal mixture on top of tart dough.
6. Bake the dish properly for fifteen to twenty minutes.
7. Dish out when the cake turns golden brown in color.
8. Garnish the icing sugar on top of the cake.
9. The dish is ready to be served.

BUBBLE TOP BROICHE

INGREDIENTS

- Two and a quarter teaspoon of active yeast
- One tablespoon of milk
- One egg
- A quarter cup of unsalted butter
- Two and a half cup of all-purpose flour
- A quarter cup of sugar
- Two cups of water
- Sea salt to taste

COOK TIME: 3 hours
SERVING: 12

INSTRUCTIONS

1. Take a mixing bowl.
2. Add the unsalted butter, all-purpose flour, sugar, active yeast and sea salt into the bowl.
3. Mix well and then add the water and milk into the bowl.
4. Knead the dough well and place it aside for two hours.
5. Take a muffin tray.
6. Cut the dough into 36 equal balls.
7. Place three balls into each muffin tray.
8. Preheat the oven at 180 degrees.
9. Place the muffin tray in the oven.
10. Bake the bread for forty minutes or until the bread turns golden brown.
11. Dish out when done.
12. Your dish is ready to be served.

SAVOURY PALMIERS WITH PARMESAN AND BLACK PEPPER

INGREDIENTS

- Half teaspoon of nutmeg
- One teaspoon of black pepper
- Three and a half cup of flour
- Half cup of parmesan cheese
- A cup of salted butter
- One tablespoon of baking powder
- Two large eggs
- Extra parmesan cheese for sprinkling
- Half teaspoon of kosher salt

COOK TIME: *20 mins*
SERVING: *4*

INSTRUCTIONS

1. Take a large bowl.
2. Add the dry ingredients in a bowl.
3. Mix all the ingredients well.
4. Add the butter and the rest of the ingredients into the bowl.
5. Add the formed mixture into a pipping bag.
6. Make small heart shaped cookies on a baking dish and sprinkle the parmesan cheese on top.
7. Bake the cookies for twenty minutes.
8. Dish out the cookies when done.
9. The dish is ready to be served.

THE SUZETTE SAUCE

INGREDIENTS

- One cup of caster sugar
- Half cup of butter
- One teaspoon of lemon zest
- Two teaspoons of orange zest
- Three tablespoons of grand Marnier
- A quarter cup of orange juice
- Two tablespoons of cognac

COOK TIME: *15 mins*
SERVING: *4*

INSTRUCTIONS

1. Take a pan.
2. Add the butter and caster sugar into the pan.
3. Cook the mixture well.
4. Add the lemon zest, orange zest, grand Marnier, cognac and orange juice into the pan.
5. Cook all the ingredients well.
6. Continue mixing until the sauce turns thick.
7. Dish out when done.
8. Your dish is ready to be served.

Chapter 5: Traditional Burgundy and Franche-Comté Recipes

Burgundy is a place where there are incredible and flavorful wines. Franche Comte and Burgundy are famous for their conventional beef bourguignon to other dishes that are cooked with lardons and red wine. All local dishes are either cooked in wine or potentially appreciated along with wine made by one of the sublime winemakers of Burgundy. Franche-comté terms with provincial specialties. It is renowned all through France for its brilliant food - a standing that is much merited! The eateries offer rich, shifted menus in light of customary plans and neighborhood produce. The food is lovely and so we will try some of the recipes belonging to these regions below.

COQ AU VIN JAUNE

INGREDIENTS

- One cup of heavy cream
- One cup of chicken pieces
- One tablespoon of kosher salt
- One tablespoon of black pepper
- Two cups of red wine
- One bay leaf
- One teaspoon of sugar
- Two thyme sprigs
- Half cup of diced bacon
- One cup of carrots
- One onions
- One teaspoon of chopped garlic
- Half cup of tomato paste
- Parsley

COOK TIME: 20 *mins*
SERVING: 2

INSTRUCTIONS

1. Take a large bowl.
2. Add the chicken pieces into it.
3. Season the chicken with pepper and salt.
4. Combine the chicken with red wine, bay leaf and thyme.
5. Cover it and marinate for thirty minutes.
6. Cook the bacons until they become crispy.
7. Add the marinated chicken into it.
8. Cook it until the chicken becomes golden brown.
9. Add the onions, carrots, and all the vegetables.
10. Add the garlic, tomato paste and cook for one minute.
11. Add the rest of the ingredients into the mixture.
12. Cook the ingredients for ten to fifteen minutes.
13. Your dish is ready to be served.

ESCALOPE DE VEAU COMTOISE

INGREDIENTS

- Two tablespoons of olive oil
- Six veal cutlets
- Six ham slices
- Salt to taste
- Black pepper to taste
- Half cup of parmesan cheese
- Two tablespoons of chopped shallots
- Two cups of mushroom slices
- A quarter cup of brandy
- One cup of heavy cream

COOK TIME: 30 mins
SERVING: 4

INSTRUCTIONS

1. Take a pan.
2. Add the olive oil, and shallots into the pan.
3. Cook the shallots until they turn soft.
4. Add the veal cutlets and ham pieces into the pan.
5. Cook well.
6. Add the mushroom slices, brandy, salt and black pepper into the pan.
7. Add the heavy cream into the pan.
8. Cook the meat pieces for ten minutes.
9. Dish out when done.
10. Garnish the dish with parmesan cheese on top.
11. Your dish is ready to be served.

RACLETTE JURASSIENNE

INGREDIENTS

- Two tablespoons of olive oil
- One cup of diced raclette cheese
- Four golden potatoes
- Salt to taste
- Black pepper to taste
- One teaspoon of mixed herb powder
- Half cup of chopped chives

COOK TIME: 30 mins
SERVING: 4

INSTRUCTIONS

1. Take a pan.
2. Add the olive oil, and potatoes into the pan.
3. Cook the potatoes until they turn soft.
4. Add salt, black pepper and mixed herb powder into the pan.
5. Cook well and dish out.
6. Place the potatoes, chopped chives and raclette cheese in a baking dish.
7. Bake the potatoes until the cheese turns soft.
8. Dish out when done.
9. Your dish is ready to be served.

POIRES AU VIN- WINE POACHED PEARS

INGREDIENTS

- One cup of red wine
- Two tablespoons of honey
- One cup of white wine
- Two cups of orange juice
- A quarter teaspoon of cinnamon powder
- One teaspoon of vanilla extract
- Half teaspoon of orange zest
- Six pears

COOK TIME: 10 mins
SERVING: 4

INSTRUCTIONS

1. Take a pan.
2. Add the red wine, white wine, honey, orange zest, orange juice and cinnamon powder into the pan.
3. Let the mixture cook well until the mixture starts boiling.
4. Add the pears into the wine mixture.
5. Coat the wine sauce all over the pears.
6. Switch off the stove.
7. Transfer the pears into serving plates.
8. Your dish is ready to be served.

TARTE AU GOUMEAU

INGREDIENTS

- One tablespoon of olive oil
- Two cups of lemon verbena
- One cup of chopped rhubarb
- Crushed black pepper to taste
- Four teaspoons of sugar
- Half teaspoon of freshly grated nutmeg
- Salt to taste
- **For dough:**
- Two cups of all-purpose flour
- Two teaspoons of fine sea salt
- Half cup of unsalted soft butter
- Two whole egg
- A quarter cup of ice water

COOK TIME: 40 mins
SERVING: 6

INSTRUCTIONS

1. Take a large bowl.
2. Add the flour and sea salt into the bowl.
3. Mix the ingredients well and add the eggs, water and softened butter into the bowl.
4. Mix all the ingredients well to form a dough.
5. Take a large pan.
6. Add the olive oil into the pan.
7. Add the chopped rhubarb when the olive oil heats well.
8. Mix the chopped rhubarb and add the sugar into the pan.
9. Cook the ingredients until the sugar is melted.
10. Add the black pepper, salt, freshly grated nutmeg and lemon verbena into the pan.
11. Cook the ingredients for about five minutes.
12. Switch off the stove and let the mixture cool down.
13. Roll out the dough and lay half of it in a tart baking dish.
14. Add the cooked mixture on the dough.
15. Bake the tart for about twenty to twenty-five minutes.
16. Dish out the tart when it is done.
17. Your dish is ready to be served.

CROUTE AU MÓNT DÓR

INGREDIENTS

- Two tablespoons of olive oil
- One cup of diced comte
- Four large pastry sheets
- Two cups of chopped figs
- Salt to taste
- Black pepper to taste
- Two tablespoons of chopped onions
- Half cup of chopped proscuitto

COOK TIME: 30 mins
SERVING: 4

INSTRUCTIONS

1. Take a pan.
2. Add the olive oil, and onions into the pan.
3. Cook the onions until they turn soft.
4. Add the chopped prosciutto into the pan.
5. Cook well and dish out.
6. Cut the pastry sheets in half.
7. Stuff the formed mixture, figs and diced comte on the pastry sheets.
8. Roll the pasty sheets and close the opened ends with a fork
9. Place the pastries on a greased baking dish.
10. Bake the pastries for thirty minutes.
11. Dish out when the pastries turn golden brown in color.
12. Your dish is ready to be served.

Chapter 6: Traditional Bordeaux, Périgord, Gascony, and Basque country Recipes

Popular for its wine, Bordeaux, Périgord, and Gascony are additionally a foodie's paradise. The Basque cooking is liberal, superb, and loaded with character, according to the domain and its occupants. The Basque cooking is inconspicuous with the impacts of the seafront and its open country. The business sectors, ranch shops, or other food shops make it simple to get the delectable items that are the focal point of numerous flavorful ordinary dishes. Following are some more delicious recipes that you will love trying!

BASQUE BRAISED CHICKEN WITH PEPPERS

INGREDIENTS

- One cup of chicken pieces
- One tablespoon of kosher salt
- One tablespoon of black pepper
- Two cups of red wine
- Two tablespoons of olive oil
- One bay leaf
- One teaspoon of sugar
- Two thyme
- One cup of carrots
- One cup of piquillo peppers
- One onions
- One tablespoon of all-purpose flour
- Two tablespoons of brandy
- One teaspoon of chopped garlic
- Parsley for garnishing

COOK TIME: *20 mins*
SERVING: *2*

INSTRUCTIONS

1. Take a large bowl.
2. Add the chicken pieces into it.
3. Season the chicken with pepper and salt.
4. Combine the chicken with red wine, bay leaf and thyme.
5. Cover it and marinate for thirty minutes.
6. Cook the piquillo peppers until they become crispy.
7. Add the marinated chicken into it.
8. Cook it until the chicken becomes golden brown.
9. Add the onions, and tomato paste into the pan.
10. Add the garlic, and all-purpose flour into the pan.
11. Cook well until the flour turns fragrant.
12. Add the brandy into the mixture.
13. Cook the dish for five more minutes and then dish out.
14. Add the chopped parsley on top and serve hot.

Tip: You can use unsalted butter instead of olive oil in this recipe.

BASQUE TUNA AND POTATO SOUP

INGREDIENTS

- Four cups of vegetable stock
- Two tablespoons of crushed garlic
- Salt to taste
- Black pepper to taste
- Two tablespoons of olive oil
- One cup of dried white wine
- One cup of onion
- One cup of tuna pieces
- Two cups of potato pieces
- One cup of diced bell pepper
- Two tablespoons of chopped fresh herbs
- One teaspoon of smoked paprika
- Chopped dill for servings

COOK TIME: 20 mins
SERVING: 4

INSTRUCTIONS

1. Take a large saucepan.
2. Add the oil and onions into the pan.
3. Cook the onions until they turn golden brown.
4. Add the crushed garlic into the pan.
5. Add the tuna pieces and potato pieces into the mixture.
6. Add the vegetable stock, smoked paprika and dried white wine.
7. Mix all the ingredients well and add the fresh herbs into the pan.
8. Cover the pan with a lid for five minutes.
9. Let the soup cook properly.
10. Season the soup with salt and black pepper.
11. Dish out the soup into soup bowls.
12. Add the chopped fresh dill on top.
13. The dish is ready to be served.

BASQUE STYLE FISH WITH GREEN PEPPERS AND MANILA CLAMS

INGREDIENTS

- A quarter cup of red wine
- One pound of boiled manila clams
- One pound of fish
- Two teaspoons of minced shallots
- Two tablespoons of lemon juice
- Two tablespoons of chopped fresh green peppers
- Salt to taste
- Black pepper

INSTRUCTIONS

1. Take a heatable bowl.
2. Add the red wine, manila clams, fish, minced shallots, lemon juice, green peppers, salt and black pepper into the bowl.
3. Bake the fish for twenty minutes at 180 degrees.
4. Mix all the ingredients well.
5. Add the mixture into a serving dish.
6. Your dish is ready to be served.

COOK TIME: *20 mins*
SERVING: *4*

CANÉLE RECIPE

INGREDIENTS

- Two cups of almond flour
- Two eggs
- One tablespoon of vanilla extract
- A cup of milk
- A tablespoon of vegetable oil
- A cup of all-purpose flour
- Half cup of whole wheat flour
- Salt to taste
- Water to knead

COOK TIME: 50 mins
SERVING: 4

INSTRUCTIONS

1. Take a bowl.
2. Add the flour into it.
3. Add the sugar into it.
4. Add lukewarm water in it.
5. Set aside for half an hour.
6. Add the whole wheat flour.
7. Add the salt and some water in it.
8. Add the eggs and vanilla extract into the mixture.
9. Add the almond flour and some of milk.
10. Mix the ingredients well so that a smooth mixture can be obtained.
11. Add the oil if required for smoothness.
12. Steam the dish in a water bath for thirty minutes.
13. Your dish is ready to be served.

CREAM PUFF

INGREDIENTS

- Half cup of whole milk
- One tablespoon of sugar
- One cup of all-purpose flour
- Two eggs
- Five tablespoons of butter
- One cup of whipped cream
- One teaspoon of vanilla extract

COOK TIME: 50 mins
SERVING: 4

INSTRUCTIONS

1. Take a saucepan and add the water in it.
2. Add the milk, butter, sugar, vanilla extract and salt into it.
3. Boil the whole mixture.
4. Add the flour into it and mix well.
5. Cook the mixture for two minutes.
6. Remove it when the dough is formed.
7. Transfer the dough into a bowl.
8. Add the eggs into it.
9. Beat the mixture until dough becomes smooth.
10. Make the puffs of desired shape.
11. Bake the puffs for twenty minutes at 160 degrees.
12. Dish out when the puffs turn golden brown in color.
13. Pipe the whipped cream in the puffs.
14. Your dish is ready to be served.

SAINT EMILION MACARON

INGREDIENTS

- One cup of almond flour
- A quarter teaspoon of cream of tartar
- One cup of superfine sugar
- One cup of egg whites
- One cup of icing sugar

COOK TIME: 20 *mins*
SERVING: 4

INSTRUCTIONS

1. Take a large bowl.
2. Add the egg whites, and salt into a bowl.
3. Beat the egg whites well until they turn stiff.
4. Add the cream of tartar and superfine sugar into the bowl.
5. Mix all the ingredients well to form a homogenous mixture.
6. Add the almond flour slowly into the egg whites' mixture.
7. Fold the mixture well.
8. Preheat the oven at 180 degrees.
9. Take a greased baking tray.
10. Pour the macaron mixture into a pipping bag.
11. Make small cookies on the baking tray.
12. Place the baking tray into the oven.
13. Bake the macarons for twenty minutes.
14. Dish out the macarons when done.
15. Let the macarons cool down.
16. Garnish the cookies with icing sugar.
17. Your dish is ready to be served.

LE PETIT SALE

INGREDIENTS

- Two strips of thyme leaves
- One cup of chopped onions
- One tablespoon of black pepper
- One cup of chopped pork
- Two tablespoons of olive oil
- Two teaspoons of chopped garlic
- One cup of red lentils
- A pinch of rosemary
- One teaspoon of black pepper
- Two cups of chicken stock
- One cup of red wine
- A pinch of salt
- One tablespoon of chopped fresh parsley

COOK TIME: *40 mins*
SERVING: *4*

INSTRUCTIONS

1. Take a large pan.
2. Add the oil and onions into the pan.
3. Cook the onions until they turn soft and translucent.
4. Add the garlic into the pan.
5. Cook the mixture well.
6. Add the pork pieces, black pepper, red wine and red wine.
7. Cook the mixture for five minutes.
8. Add the salt, rosemary, and thyme into the pan.
9. Cook the ingredients well.
10. Add the chicken stock into the pan.
11. Cover the pan and cook for twenty minutes.
12. Garnish the dish with chopped fresh parsley.
13. Your dish is ready to be served.

FRENCH BISTRO SALAD

INGREDIENTS

- Three cups of rocket leaves
- Two cups of watercress salad
- One cup of bacon lardon
- Half cup of fresh thyme
- Half teaspoon of smoked paprika
- Half cup of chopped chives
- Two tablespoons of olive oil
- Half cup of Dijon mustard
- Two boiled eggs

COOK TIME: 10 mins
SERVING: 2

INSTRUCTIONS

1. Take a pan.
2. Add the olive oil and bacon lardon into the pan.
3. Cook the bacon lardon well.
4. Dish out when the bacon is done.
5. Take a large bowl.
6. Add the Dijon mustard, and paprika into a bowl.
7. Mix all the ingredients well to form a homogenous mixture.
8. Add the bacon lardon, rocket leaves, watercress salad, fresh thyme and chopped chives on top of the mixture.
9. Toss the salad to make sure everything is mixed properly.
10. Your dish is ready to be served.

CHERRY CLAFOUTIS

INGREDIENTS

- Two cups of milk
- A teaspoon of cinnamon
- Half cup of heavy cream
- Half cup of white sugar
- A teaspoon of salt
- Two eggs
- A teaspoon of lemon extract
- A teaspoon of almond extract
- Two cups of all-purpose flour
- A cup of butter
- A cup of pitted cherries

COOK TIME: *10 mins*
SERVING: *4*

INSTRUCTIONS

1. Take a medium bowl.
2. Add the melted butter in it.
3. Add the heavy cream and cinnamon into it.
4. Add the flour into the bowl and mix well.
5. Add the milk and salt into the bowl.
6. Add the sugar into the bowl.
7. Mix them well.
8. Add the eggs, cherries, lemon extract and almond extract together.
9. Stir the mixture for few minutes.
10. Add the clafoutis material on baking sheet.
11. Bake the material for twenty minutes until they become slightly brown.
12. Your dish is ready to be served.

SASKATOON CLAFOUTIS

INGREDIENTS

- Two cups of milk
- A teaspoon of cinnamon
- Half cup of heavy cream
- Half cup of white sugar
- A teaspoon of salt
- Two eggs
- A teaspoon of lemon extract
- A teaspoon of almond extract
- Two cups of all-purpose flour
- A cup of butter
- A cup of pitted Saskatoon berries

COOK TIME: 10 mins
SERVING: 4

INSTRUCTIONS

1. Take a medium bowl.
2. Add the melted butter in it.
3. Add the heavy cream and cinnamon into it.
4. Add the flour and mix well.
5. Add the milk and salt into the bowl.
6. Add the sugar into the bowl.
7. Mix them well.
8. Add the eggs, Saskatoon berry, lemon extract and almond extract together.
9. Stir the mixture for few minutes.
10. Add the clafoutis material on baking sheet.
11. Bake the material for twenty minutes until they become slightly brown.
12. Your dish is ready to be served.

Chapter 7: Traditional Provence-Alpes-Côte d'Azur Recipes

Food and gastronomy in Provence-Alpes-Côte d'Azur significantly influence the territorial lifestyle. This tremendous Mediterranean locale is generally famous for ideal harmony between Spanish, Italian, and French gastronomies. Aside from flaunting beautiful seashores, extravagant manors, and radiant climate, this piece of the South of France, to be sure, offers pleasant and vivid food. This chapter contains ten delicious recipes from Provence that you need to try!

PROVENCAL BEEF STEW

INGREDIENTS

- Two bay leaves
- One cup of chopped onions
- One tablespoon of black pepper
- One cup of chopped leek
- Two tablespoons of olive oil
- Two teaspoons of chopped garlic
- One cup of beef chunks
- One cup of tomato paste
- A pinch of saffron
- One teaspoon of black pepper
- Two cups of ripe tomatoes
- Two cups of beef stock
- Two tablespoons of Pernod
- A pinch of salt
- One tablespoon of chopped fresh chives

COOK TIME: *20 mins*
SERVING: *4*

INSTRUCTIONS

1. Take a large pan.
2. Add the oil and onions into the pan.
3. Cook the onions until they turn soft and translucent.
4. Add the garlic into the pan.
5. Cook the mixture well.
6. Add the tomato paste, chopped ripe tomatoes and spices.
7. Cook the mixture for five minutes.
8. Add the beef chunks into the pan.
9. Cook the ingredients well.
10. Add the beef stock, chopped leeks, and pernod.
11. Cover the pan and cook for ten minutes.
12. Garnish the dish with chopped fresh chives.
13. Your dish is ready to be served.

FRENCH ANCHOIADE

INGREDIENTS

- Two cups of minced anchovies
- A pinch of kosher salt
- A quarter cup of olive oil
- Two tablespoons of minced garlic
- Half teaspoon of Dijon mustard
- Black pepper to taste

COOK TIME: *15 mins*
SERVING: *4*

INSTRUCTIONS

1. Take a pan.
2. Add the olive oil and minced garlic into the pan.
3. Cook the garlic well.
4. Add the Dijon mustard, black pepper, kosher salt, and minced anchovies into the pan.
5. Cook all the ingredients well.
6. Continue mixing until the sauce turns thick.
7. Dish out when done.
8. Your dish is ready to be served.

SWEET CHARD PIE

INGREDIENTS

- One tablespoon of olive oil
- A quarter cup of parmesan cheese
- Half cup of chopped red onion
- Two cups of fresh chopped sweet chard
- Crushed black pepper to taste
- Half teaspoon of freshly grated nutmeg
- Salt to taste
- **For dough:**
- Two cups of all-purpose flour
- Two teaspoons of fine sea salt
- Half cup of unsalted soft butter
- Two whole egg
- A quarter cup of ice water

COOK TIME: 40 mins
SERVING: 6

INSTRUCTIONS

1. Take a large bowl.
2. Add the flour and sea salt into the bowl.
3. Mix the ingredients well and add the eggs, water and softened butter into the bowl.
4. Mix all the ingredients well to form a dough.
5. Take a large pan.
6. Add the olive oil into the pan.
7. Add the onions when the olive oil heats well.
8. Mix the onions and add the chopped sweet chard into the pan.
9. Cook the ingredients until the spinach is wilted.
10. Add the parmesan cheese, black pepper, salt, and freshly grated nutmeg into the pan.
11. Cook the ingredients for about five minutes.
12. Switch off the stove and let the mixture cool down.
13. Roll out the dough and lay half of it in a round baking dish.
14. Add the cooked mixture on the dough and cover the mixture with rest of the dough.
15. Bake the pie for about twenty to twenty-five minutes.
16. Dish out the pie when it is done.
17. Your dish is ready to be served.

SOCCA NICOISE FLATBREAD

INGREDIENTS

- One cup of butter
- Four whole egg
- Half cup of olive oil
- A pinch of salt
- One cup of finely chopped onion
- Four cups of chickpea flour

COOK TIME: 40 mins
SERVING: 4

INSTRUCTIONS

1. Take a large bowl.
2. Add the eggs, chickpea flour, onion, olive oil and salt into the bowl.
3. Knead the mixture well to form a dough.
4. Preheat the oven at 180 degrees.
5. Divide the dough into four pieces.
6. Roll out each of the dough.
7. Take a greased baking dish.
8. Place the rolled dough into the dish.
9. Place the baking dish into the oven.
10. Bake the dough for forty minutes.
11. Dish out the bread when done.
12. Your dish is ready to be served.

AUBERGINE & COURGETTE TIAN

INGREDIENTS

- Kosher salt to taste
- Black pepper to taste
- One cup of eggplant pieces
- One cup of zucchini pieces
- One cup of chopped chives
- One cup of cherry tomatoes
- Half cup of summer savory sprigs
- Two tablespoons of minced garlic
- Two tablespoons of dried thyme
- Half cup of chopped parsley
- Two teaspoons of Herbs de Provence
- Half cup of chopped onion
- Two tablespoons of olive oil
- Half cup of basil leaves
- One cup of red bell pepper
- One tablespoon of crushed red pepper

COOK TIME: 30 mins
SERVING: 4

INSTRUCTIONS

1. Preheat the oven at 150 degrees.
2. Take a large pan.
3. Add the olive oil and chopped onions into it.
4. Cook the onions until they turn light brown in color.
5. Add the minced garlic into the pan.
6. Cook the mixture for five minutes.
7. Season the mixture with salt and pepper.
8. Add the spices.
9. Add the cherry tomatoes in a bowl and add the salt.
10. Dish the mixture out in a bowl.
11. Add the vegetable pieces one by one and form a design into a baking pan.
12. Pour the tomato mixture on top.
13. Add the basil and parsley leaves on top and bake the mixture for ten to fifteen minutes.
14. Dish out when done.
15. Your dish is ready to be served.

SPINACH BAKE

INGREDIENTS

- Two tablespoons of olive oil
- Two teaspoons of chopped garlic
- Two cups of chopped spinach
- Two tablespoons of chopped fresh herbs
- Salt to taste
- Black pepper to taste
- Two tablespoons of chopped onions
- One cup of heavy cream
- Half cup of mozzarella cheese

COOK TIME: *30 mins*
SERVING: *4*

INSTRUCTIONS

1. Preheat the oven at 180 degrees.
2. Take a pan.
3. Add the chopped spinach, heavy cream, chopped garlic, olive oil, and onions in the pan.
4. Mix well.
5. Season the mixture with salt and black pepper.
6. Pour the spinach in a greased baking pan.
7. Sprinkle the mozzarella cheese on top.
8. Bake the spinach for thirty minutes.
9. Dish out when done.
10. Your dish is ready to be served.

VAUCLUSE TROUT

INGREDIENTS

- Kosher salt to taste
- Black pepper to taste
- One cup of trout fillet pieces
- A quarter cup of sliced almonds
- One cup of chopped chives
- Two tablespoons of dried thyme
- Half cup of chopped parsley
- Two tablespoons of olive oil

COOK TIME: 30 mins
SERVING: 4

INSTRUCTIONS

1. Take a large pan.
2. Add the olive oil and trout pieces into the pan.
3. Cook the trout pieces until they turn light brown in color.
4. Add the chopped chives and dried thyme into the pan.
5. Cook the mixture for five minutes.
6. Season the mixture with salt and pepper.
7. Add the almonds into the pan.
8. Cook the mixture for about ten to fifteen minutes.
9. Dish out when done.
10. Your dish is ready to be served.

FRESH FRENCH GOAT CHEESE DIP

INGREDIENTS

- One cup of chopped goat cheese
- Three tablespoons of minced garlic
- One cup of parmesan cheese
- One teaspoon of salt
- Two tablespoons of parsley
- A quarter cup of olive oil
- Two tablespoons of lime juice
- A quarter cup of fresh oregano
- Black pepper to taste
- Toasted bread for serving

COOK TIME: *20 mins*
SERVING: *4*

INSTRUCTIONS

1. Heat a stockpot over medium-high heat.
2. Add the parmesan cheese and goat cheese into the pot.
3. Cook and twenty minutes, or until the cheeses melt.
4. Add the cheese into a blender once done.
5. Add the parsley, lime juice, fresh oregano, minced garlic, salt, olive oil, and black pepper into the blender.
6. Blend everything well and dish it out in a bowl.
7. Your dish is ready to be served with toasted bread on the side.

POTATO AND MINT RAVIOLI

INGREDIENTS

- One tablespoon of olive oil
- One tablespoon of fresh rosemary leaves
- Two chicken stock cubes
- One chopped onion
- One and a half cup of boiled potato ravioli
- A quarter cup of chopped mint
- Half cup of Parmesan cheese
- Five cups of water

COOK TIME: 35 mins
SERVING: 4

INSTRUCTIONS

1. Take a sauce pan.
2. Add the water and stock cubes into the sauce pan.
3. Let the water boil until only one cup of water remains.
4. Place the water aside.
5. Take a pan.
6. Add the olive oil and onions into the pan.
7. Cook the onions until they turn soft.
8. Add the ravioli into the pan.
9. Cook the ravioli well for ten to fifteen minutes until they turn soft.
10. Season the ravioli with salt and pepper.
11. Add the fresh rosemary leaves into the pan.
12. Now slowly add the stock water into the ravioli mixture.
13. Make sure you continuously keep on mixing the ravioli.
14. Add the mint and parmesan cheese into the pan.
15. Cook the ingredients until done
16. Dish out and serve hot.

LARDON AND OLIVE CAKE

INGREDIENTS

- One cup of butter
- One cup of bacon lardons
- One teaspoon of baking soda
- Two teaspoons of baking powder
- Four whole egg
- Half cup of olive oil
- A quarter cup of pitted green olives
- A pinch of salt
- One and a half cup of all-purpose flour

COOK TIME: 40 mins
SERVING: 12

INSTRUCTIONS

1. Take a large bowl.
2. Add the eggs, baking powder, all-purpose flour, bacon lardons, green olives, baking soda, butter and salt into the bowl.
3. Knead the mixture well to form a dough.
4. Preheat the oven at 180 degrees.
5. Take a greased baking dish.
6. Add the dough mixture into the dish.
7. Place the baking dish into the oven.
8. Bake the dough for forty minutes.
9. Dish out the cake when done.
10. Your dish is ready to be served.

Chapter 8: Traditional Corsica Recipes

The hilly inside of Corsica is critical to understanding the island's culinary inclinations. Green fields are great for sheep raising, forested slopes stir with unfenced pigs and wild hog drawn by a perpetual stock of flavor-giving chestnuts, trout fishes fished out of clean-water streams, honey bees flourish with plenty of blossoms, and mushrooms give a pre-winter abundance to match the extravagant spring. Corsican cuisine is a portion of delicious and liberal food that you need to try!

CORSICAN VEAL AND OLIVE STEW

INGREDIENTS

- Four cups of vegetable stock
- Two tablespoons of crushed garlic
- Salt to taste
- Black pepper to taste
- Two tablespoons of olive oil
- One cup of onion
- One cup of diced veal pieces
- One cup of pitted green olives
- One bouillon cube
- Two tablespoons of chopped fresh herbs

COOK TIME: 20 *mins*
SERVING: 4

INSTRUCTIONS

1. Take a large saucepan.
2. Add the oil and onions into the pan.
3. Cook the onions until they turn golden brown.
4. Add the crushed garlic into the pan.
5. Add the veal and olives into the mixture.
6. Add the vegetable stock and bouillon cube into the pan.
7. Mix all the ingredients well and add the fresh herbs into the pan.
8. Cover the pan with a lid for five minutes.
9. Let the soup cook properly.
10. Season the soup with salt and black pepper.
11. Dish out the soup.
12. The dish is ready to be served.

CANNELLONI BROCCIU

INGREDIENTS

- One cup of chopped onion
- One tablespoon of fresh dill
- Four teaspoons of olive oil
- One teaspoon of dried oregano
- Two cloves of chopped garlic
- Two cups of tomato paste
- Half cup of chopped parsley leaves
- One cup of crumbled brocciu
- One pack of boiled cannelloni tubes
- One cup of ground beef
- One teaspoon of salt
- One teaspoon of black pepper

COOK TIME: 30 *mins*
SERVING: 4

INSTRUCTIONS

1. Preheat the oven at 160 degrees.
2. Take a large pan.
3. Add the olive oil and onion.
4. Cook the onions until they turn soft.
5. Add the garlic into the pan.
6. Cook for about two to three minutes.
7. Add the beef and spices.
8. Mix well and then add the tomato paste.
9. Cook the ingredients well for ten minutes.
10. Take a baking dish and place some of the beef paste on it.
11. Fill the cannelloni tubes with the cooked beef mixture and brocciu cheese on top.
12. Make similar layers until all the ingredients finish.
13. Add the chopped parsley leaves on top.
14. Bake the dish for about twenty minutes.
15. The dish is ready to be served.

CORSICAN LEMON CHEESECAKE

INGREDIENTS

- Two cups of cream cheese
- One tablespoon of vanilla essence
- One teaspoon of lemon zest
- Half cup of lemon juice
- One pack of semi crushed biscuits
- Half cup of soft cheese
- Three whole eggs
- Half cup of melted butter
- Half cup of caster sugar

COOK TIME: 20 *mins*
SERVING: 4

INSTRUCTIONS

1. Take a mixing bowl.
2. Add the cream cheese, cheese, sugar, and egg into the bowl.
3. Mix well until the mixture turns light and fluffy.
4. Add the vanilla essence, lemon zest and lemon juice into the mixture.
5. Mix well.
6. Take a baking dish.
7. Add the butter and crushed biscuits in the bottom of the dish and press the mixture well.
8. Pour the cheese mixture on top of the biscuit crust.
9. Place the dish in the oven for about twenty minutes.
10. Dish out when the cheese cake turns golden brown in color.
11. Your dish is ready to be served.

CORSICAN OMELETTE

INGREDIENTS

- Two tablespoons of butter
- Half cup of chopped mint leaves
- A pinch of salt
- A pinch of black pepper
- Half cup of grated brocciu or goat cheese
- Four eggs

COOK TIME: 15 mins
SERVING: 2

INSTRUCTIONS

1. Take a bowl.
2. Add the chopped mint leaves, eggs, salt, black pepper, and grated cheese into the bowl.
3. Mix the ingredients well.
4. Take a large pan.
5. Add the butter and let it meltdown.
6. Add in the egg mixture.
7. Cook the eggs until they turn light golden in color.
8. Dish out the omelet when done.
9. Your dish is ready to be served.

CORSICAN BISCUITS

INGREDIENTS

- Half cup of olive oil
- Half cup of almond flour
- A quarter cup of dry white wine
- Half cup of whole wheat flour
- Three teaspoons of baking powder
- One cup of raisins or nuts
- A quarter cup of brown sugar

COOK TIME: *20 mins*
SERVING: *6*

INSTRUCTIONS

1. Take a large bowl.
2. Add the olive oil, almond flour, white wine, wheat flour and brown sugar into the bowl.
3. Mix all the ingredients well to form a homogenous mixture.
4. Add the baking powder and raisins into mixture.
5. Fold the mixture well.
6. Preheat the oven at 180 degrees.
7. Take a greased baking tray.
8. Make the biscuits using pipping bag on the tray.
9. Place the baking tray into the oven.
10. Bake the biscuits for twenty minutes.
11. Dish out the biscuits when done.
12. Your dish is ready to be served.

MUSHROOM PATE

INGREDIENTS

- Two tablespoons of butter
- Two cups of mushroom mince
- Half teaspoon of thyme
- A pinch of salt
- A pinch of black pepper
- Two tablespoons of chopped almonds
- Half cup of balsamic vinegar
- One cup of chopped onion
- Half tablespoon of chopped garlic

COOK TIME: *30 mins*
SERVING: *4*

INSTRUCTIONS

1. Take a large pan.
2. Add the butter into the pan.
3. Add the onions and mushroom mince into the pan.
4. Cook the mince well.
5. Add the salt, black pepper, and thyme into the pan.
6. Cook the ingredients well.
7. Add the chopped garlic into the pan.
8. Add the balsamic vinegar and chopped almonds into the pan.
9. Cook the ingredients well.
10. Place a lid on top of the pan.
11. Cook the pate for ten to fifteen minutes.
12. Dish out when the pate is done.
13. Your dish is ready to be served.

Conclusion

The French love to eat out, so there are bistros, bars, street-side cafes, and restaurants everywhere. There are many traditional dishes in France, some of which you may be familiar with because they are popular worldwide. This cookbook incorporates creative recipes including Paris, Île-de-France, Champagne, Lorraine, Alsace, Normandy, Brittany, Loire Valley, Central France, Burgundy, Franche-Comté, Bordeaux, Périgord, Gascony, Basque country, Provence-Alpes-Côte d'Azur, and Corsica categories. So, start cooking today with this delicious French cookbook!

Printed by Amazon Italia Logistica S.r.l.
Torrazza Piemonte (TO), Italy

53322720R00067